XTREME INSECTS

BUTTERFLIES
BY S.L. HAMILTON

A&D Xtreme
An imprint of Abdo Publishing | abdobooks.com

abdobooks.com

Published by Abdo Publishing, a division of ABDO, PO Box 398166, Minneapolis, Minnesota 55439. Copyright ©2019 by Abdo Consulting Group, Inc. International copyrights reserved in all countries. No part of this book may be reproduced in any form without written permission from the publisher. A&D Xtreme™ is a trademark and logo of Abdo Publishing.

Printed in the United States of America, North Mankato, MN.
122018
012019

THIS BOOK CONTAINS RECYCLED MATERIALS

Editor: John Hamilton
Copy Editor: Bridget O'Brien
Graphic Design: Sue Hamilton
Cover Design: Laura Mitchell and Pakou Moua
Cover Photo: Minden Pictures
Interior Photos & Illustrations: Alamy-pgs 16-17; iStock-pgs 10-11, 18-19, 23 (top left & right), 24, 25 (top & bottom) & 27 (top & bottom left); Minden Pictures-pg 26 (bottom); Randwanul Hasan Siddique, KIT-pg 20 (inset); Sangay National Park-Ecuador-pg 14 (inset); Science Source-pgs 22, 28 & 29 (top right & bottom); Selena Connealy-pg 13 (bottom); Shutterstock-pgs 1, 2-3, 4-5, 6-7, 8-9, 12, 13 (top), 14, 15, 19 (inset), 20-21, 23 (bottom), 25 (middle), 26 (top), 27 (bottom right & bottom inset), 29 (top left), 30-31 & 32.

Library of Congress Control Number: 2018949999
Publisher's Cataloging-in-Publication Data

Names: Hamilton, S.L., author.
Title: Butterflies / by S.L. Hamilton.
Description: Minneapolis, Minnesota : Abdo Publishing, 2019 | Series: Xtreme insects | Includes online resources and index.
Identifiers: ISBN 9781532118159 (lib. bdg.) | ISBN 9781532171338 (ebook)
Subjects: LCSH: Butterflies--Juvenile literature. | Butterflies--Behavior--Juvenile literature. | Butterflies--Life cycles--Juvenile literature. | Insects--Juvenile literature.
Classification: DDC 595.789--dc23

CONTENTS

Butterflies 4
Metamorphosis 6
Body Parts 8
Largest Butterflies 10
Smallest Butterflies 12
Longest Proboscis 14
Flight Speed. 16
Longest Migration 18
Hiding in Plain Sight. 20
Butterfly Families 22
Can You Eat Them? 28
Glossary 30
Online Resources 31
Index 32

BUTTERFLIES

There are more than 18,000 species of butterflies on the planet. They are found on every continent except Antarctica. Butterflies come in many colors, shapes, and sizes. All of them have clear wings, but most are covered by thousands of tiny scales. The scales give them their colors. Some butterflies look like simple brown leaves, while others have a brilliant metallic shine. Butterflies help pollinate plants. A healthy population of butterflies usually means a healthy ecosystem.

Emerald Swallowtail
(Papilio palinurus)

XTREME FACT – A group of butterflies is called a flutter.

METAMORPHOSIS

The life cycle of a butterfly takes place quickly. The metamorphosis, or change, occurs in four stages and takes about a month.

BUTTERFLY LIFE CYCLE STAGES:

1) *Egg* – Tiny eggs are laid on plants. In 3-5 days, the eggs hatch.

2) *Larva* – A newborn begins life by eating its eggshell and the leaf on which it was born. It is only about the size of a pinhead. After eating constantly and molting, it will become a grown caterpillar in 9-14 days.

Larva

3) Pupa – The caterpillar attaches itself to a plant, hanging upside down. It sheds its skin one last time, covering itself in its casing, or chrysalis. It will go through its metamorphosis in the chrysalis for 10-14 days.

Adult

Pupa in Chrysalis

4) Adult – The adult emerges from the chrysalis and looks for a mate. Most butterflies only live about 2-6 weeks, so they must reproduce quickly.

BODY PARTS

Like all insects, butterflies have three main parts: the head, thorax, and abdomen. They have six legs. Butterflies are part of the Lepidoptera order, which also includes moths. The scientific name is Greek for "scale wing."

Antennae – The long antennae end with a bulb shape at the top. This helps identify butterflies from moths, which do not have this feature.

Head

Thorax

Compound Eyes The large eyes see colors extremely well, which helps it to find flowers.

Proboscis The straw-like tongue unrolls to soak up nectar.

Legs The legs have bristly hairs that are smell and taste sensors.

Hooks at the end of the legs help the butterfly to hold onto a flower or other perch.

8

Wings – Butterflies have two forewings and two hindwings. The four wings are usually covered in thousands of tiny colored scales.

The butterfly's four wings flap in an odd figure-eight pattern. This causes it to fly in an unpredictable, fluttery style that confuses predators.

Abdomen – A butterfly has 10 segments in its abdomen. Many male and female butterfly species look very different from each other. This is called being dimorphic.

XTREME FACT – Because a butterfly's wings are so big, it can fly with two of them missing.

LARGEST BUTTERFLIES

The Queen Alexandra's birdwing *(Ornithoptera alexandrae)* is the largest butterfly in the world. It is found in Papua New Guinea. It was discovered in 1906 and named after the queen of Denmark. This huge butterfly has a wingspan reaching 9.8 inches (25 cm). That's slightly smaller than a dinner plate! Its body length is 3.1 inches (8 cm). It is one of the few butterflies listed as endangered. This is mostly due to a loss of its old-growth rainforest habitat, but also because collectors want the rare butterfly.

Queen Alexandra's Birdwing
(Ornithoptera alexandrae)

SMALLEST BUTTERFLIES

The smallest butterfly in the world is the western pygmy-blue *(Brephidium exilis)*. The tiny insect has a wingspan of .5-.8 inches (12-20 mm) and is only .6 inches (1.5 cm) long. It is found in the western United States and down through Mexico to northern South America.

Western Pygmy-Blue
(Brephidium exilis)

Blue scales are seen on the open wings of a western pygmy-blue butterfly.

XTREME FACT – The western pygmy-blue uses ants as bodyguards. As a tiny caterpillar, it has a honey gland that oozes a liquid that ants find very tasty. The ants protect the small caterpillar that provides them with the sugary treat.

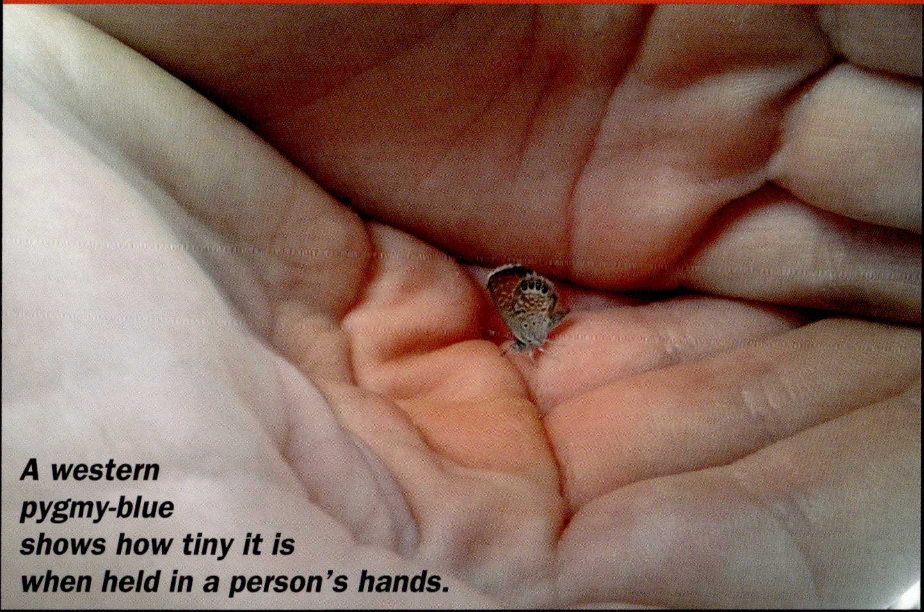

A western pygmy-blue shows how tiny it is when held in a person's hands.

13

LONGEST PROBOSCIS

Damas immaculata

The longest proboscis, relative to a butterfly's overall size, belongs to *Damas immaculata* of South America. It has a 2-inch (52-mm) proboscis. That is more than twice as long as its .9-inch (22 mm) -long body! A long proboscis allows the butterfly to reach nectar in flowers that other insects cannot. However, a butterfly must land to eat, so its proboscis cannot be too long or it will not be able to fully unroll the spongy, tonguelike tube.

← *A butterfly's proboscis collects nectar.*

Bluebottles, or blue triangles *(Graphium sarpedon)*, drink from a mud puddle for nutrients. This is sometimes called "mud-puddling."

Butterflies are known to go "puddling." They need more nutrients than they get from nectar. To get salt and other minerals, they unroll their proboscises into mud puddles, gooey poop, pee, blood, rotting fruit, and even tears and human sweat.

A red admiral *(Vanessa atalanta)* sucks up minerals from a person's sweat.

FLIGHT SPEED

Skipper butterflies are more plain looking than their brightly colored family members, but they are the fastest butterflies. There are about 3,500 species of skippers. They are known for their quick, darting flight. They are a blur of browns and grays, flying at a rate of 37 miles per hour (60 kph). That's nearly as fast as a greyhound dog can run! Most butterflies flutter more calmly through the air at a rate of 5-12 miles per hour (8-19 kph).

A high-speed camera captures a small skipper *(Thymelicus sylvestris)* in flight.

XTREME FACT – Skippers have short, plump bodies and small wings compared to other butterflies. But they have very strong wing muscles in their thorax that results in their fast flight speed.

LONGEST MIGRATION

Monarchs of North America's Great Lakes region migrate in the fall to Mexico and parts of Southern California. This is a trip of up to 3,000 miles (4,828 km). Offspring of these butterflies will fly back north in the spring.

Monarch butterflies (Danaus plexippus) migrate to where it is warm. They fly to the same tree in the same location every year, even though it's a different generation that has never been there before.

XTREME FACT – Painted ladies (*Vanessa cardui*) migrate from southern Europe to Africa in the fall. This is the longest butterfly migration, a trip of 3,750 miles (6,035 km). The offspring fly back to Europe in spring.

HIDING IN PLAIN SIGHT

A glasswing butterfly *(Greta oto)* has no scales on parts of its wings. The see-through wings act as camouflage for the butterfly. It is hard for a predator to see where the butterfly is when it blends in with the sky or whatever it lands on.

How clear are a glasswing's wings? A person can read words through the scaleless parts!

XTREME FACT – A glasswing caterpillar has hairy projections that make it unappealing to predators.

Glasswing
(Greta oto)

BUTTERFLY FAMILIES

Butterflies are divided into six families. Each one has unique traits. The number of members in each family changes as new butterflies are discovered and others die out.

BRUSH-FOOTED BUTTERFLIES

Brush-footed (Family: Nymphalidae) are the largest butterfly family with more than 6,000 members. They have smaller-sized front legs that they hold up. These legs look like brushes, which gives them their common name. They walk on their four back legs.

White Peacock
(*Anartia jatrophae*)

Front Legs

GOSSAMER-WINGED BUTTERFLIES

Gossamer-winged (Family: Lycaenidae) are the second-largest family of butterflies, with nearly 6,000 species. They are also called blues, hairstreaks, and coppers. They are small, bright-colored butterflies with a metallic gloss to their delicate-looking (gossamer) wings.

Purple-Edged Copper (Lycaena hippothoe)

Common Blue (Polyommatus icarus)

Gray Hairstreak (Strymon melinus)

Some members of the Lycaenidae family have hairlike tail projections that look like antennae. A predator sees them and attacks the other side, thinking it's sneaking up on the butterfly. But the butterfly sees it coming and escapes.

23

SKIPPERS

Skippers (Family: Hesperiidae) are known for their quick, darting flight patterns. There are about 3,500 species of them. They have unique antenna tips that end in a narrow hook, rather than the bulb-shaped tips that are found on other butterflies.

Hooklike antenna tips.

Long-Tailed Skipper (*Urbanus proteus*)

24

SWALLOWTAILS & PARNASSIANS

Swallowtails (Family: Papilionidae) have forked tails that look much like the swallow, a common bird. There are about 480 species of swallowtails.

Eastern Tiger Swallowtail (*Papilio glaucus*)

All Papilionidae caterpillars have an osmeterium. The forklike organ pops out from the thorax when they feel threatened. It gives off a terrible-smelling liquid that repels attackers such as ants, spiders, and mantises.

Parnassians do not have forked tails like their family members. They are mostly a high-altitude butterfly found in arctic and mountainous regions. Their dark bodies help warm them. There are about 50 species.

Mountain Apollo (*Parnassius apollo*)

25

METALMARKS

Metalmarks (Family: Riodinidae) are named for the metallic-looking spots on their wings. Many of them mimic the look of poisonous moths to protect themselves from predators. Males have much shorter front legs and do not use them for walking. There are more than 1,500 species.

Banded Red Harlequin
(Paralaxita orphna)

Metalmark males have short front legs.

Green Mantle
(Caria lampeto)

Metalmarks are known for their metallike scales.

WHITES, YELLOWS, AND SULPHURS

Whites, yellows, and sulphurs (Family: Pieridae) are named for their white, yellow, and orange colors. There are about 1,100 species.

**Black-Veined White
(*Aporia crataegi*)**

**Clouded Yellow
(*Colias croceus*)**

**Orange-Barred Sulphur
(*Phoebis philea*)**

XTREME FACT – The word "butterfly," may have come from the Pieridae species. Scientists called the common brimstone butterfly Gonepteryx rhamni. This translates to "butter-colored fly."

27

CAN YOU EAT THEM?

People can eat the larva stage (caterpillars) of some butterflies. They are a good source of protein. Brush-footed butterfly larvae are eaten in the Congo and other African countries. Humans do not eat adult butterflies since the insects are covered in hairs and scales. Butterflies may also have a toxic dust in their wings. If eaten, it makes people sick. Even predators do not eat the wings.

A mantis eats the abdomen of an adult butterfly.

A blue-throated bee-eater bird with a butterfly meal.

A green lynx spider captures a butterfly.

Eggs, larvae, pupae, and adult butterflies are tasty meals for a variety of wildlife in the air, on land, and in the water. Birds, spiders, frogs, toads, lizards, snakes, fish, wasps, ants, and even some monkeys, mice, and rats enjoy a butterfly lunch.

A harvest mouse feeds on a monarch butterfly.

GLOSSARY

Antennae
Long, thin appendages on an insect's head that act as sensors for such things as vibrations or scents.

Compound Eyes
Eyes made up of thousands of lenses. These types of eyes have excellent vision and can easily detect movement. Butterflies have 6,000 lenses in each eye. Humans have 1 lens per eye.

Ecosystem
A biological community of animals, plants, and bacteria that live together in the same physical or chemical environment.

Great Lakes Region
An area in North America that includes parts of eight U.S. states: Illinois, Indiana, Michigan, Minnesota, New York, Ohio, Pennsylvania, and Wisconsin, as well as Canada's Ontario province.

Larvae
Newly hatched insects that have not changed into the adult form.

Molt
Insects shed, or molt, their outer layer in order to grow bigger. Many insects molt several times before reaching adulthood.

Nectar
A sugary liquid produced by plants and found in flowers, that butterflies eat as food. Bees collect it to make honey.

Nutrients
Materials in food that are needed for healthy growth. This includes vitamins, minerals, and proteins.

Species
A group of living things that have similar looks and behaviors, but are not identical. They are often called by a similar name. For example, there are about 18,000 species of butterflies.

Toxic
A poison that causes living things to sicken and sometimes die.

ONLINE RESOURCES

Booklinks NONFICTION NETWORK
FREE! ONLINE NONFICTION RESOURCES

To learn more about butterflies, visit abdobooklinks.com. These links are routinely monitored and updated to provide the most current information available.

INDEX

A
Africa 19, 28
Anartia jatropha (*see* white peacock)
Antarctica 4
Aporia crataegi (*see* black-veined white)

B
banded red harlequin 26
black-veined white 27
blue triangles (*see also* bluebottles) 15
bluebottles (*see also* blue triangles) 15
blues 23
Brephidium exilis (*see* western pygmy-blue)
brush-footed butterflies 22, 28

C
California, Southern 18
Caria lampeto (*see* green mantle)
clouded yellow 27
Colias croceus (*see* clouded yellow)
common blue 23
common brimstone 27
Congo 28
coppers 23

D
Damas immaculata 14
Danaus plexippus (*see* monarch)
Denmark 10

E
eastern tiger swallowtail 25
emerald swallowtail 5
Europe 19

G
glasswing 20, 21
Gonepteryx rhamni (*see* common brimstone)
gossamer-winged butterflies 23
Graphium sarpedon (*see* blue triangles and bluebottles)

gray hairstreak 23
Great Lakes region 18
green mantle 26
Greta oto (*see* glasswing)

H
hairstreaks 23
Hesperiidae (*see* skippers)

L
Lepidoptera order 8
long-tailed skipper 24
Lycaena hippothoe (*see* purple-edged copper)
Lycaenidae (*see* gossamer-winged butterflies)

M
metalmarks 26
Mexico 12, 18
monarch 18
mountain Apollo 25

N
North America 18
Nymphalidae (*see* brush-footed butterflies)

O
orange-barred sulphur 27
Ornithoptera alexandrae (*see* Queen Alexandra's birdwing)

P
painted lady 19
Papilio glaucus (*see* eastern tiger swallowtail)
Papilio palinurus (*see* emerald swallowtail)
Papilionidae (*see* swallowtails and parnassians)
Papua New Guinea 10
Paralaxita orphna (*see* banded red harlequin)
parnassians 25
Parnassius apollo (*see* mountain Apollo)
Phoebis philea (*see* orange-barred sulphur)
Pieridae (*see* whites, yellows, and sulphurs)

Polyommatus icarus (*see* common blue)
purple-edged copper 23

Q
Queen Alexandra's birdwing 10, 11

R
red admiral 15
Riodinidae (*see* metalmarks)

S
skippers 16, 17, 24
small skipper 17
South America 12, 14
Strymon melinus (*see* gray hairstreak)
sulphurs 27
swallowtails 25

T
Thymelicus sylvestris (*see* small skipper)

U
United States 12
Urbanus proteus (*see* long-tailed skipper)

V
Vanessa atalanta (*see* red admiral)
Vanessa cardui (*see* painted lady)

W
western pygmy-blue 12, 13
white peacock 22
whites 27

Y
yellows 27